My Ten Legged Journey

The Road to Rainbow Bridge

Shirl Knobloch

...

My Ten Legged Journey: The Road to Rainbow Bridge

Edited by: Jennifer Sabatelli

Cover, Photography, and Artwork by: Shirl Knobloch

ISBN 13: 978-0-9974752-1-0

Also by Shirl Knobloch:

- *Birdsong, Barks, and Banter: Adventures of an Animal Intuitive Reiki Master and Her Home of Misfit Companions*

- *The Returning Ones: A Medium's Memoirs*

- *You're Never Too Old for Fairy Tales*

- *Reenactments from My Heart: Spiritual and Supernatural Civil War Fiction and Poetry*

- *Once Upon a Fairy Tale*

- *Strength of a Lion, Soul of a Lamb: A Collection of Wolfhound Fairy Tales and Poetry*

• • •

For every paw print on my heart--

From my Snoopy, the first, and for every paw that walked in

after him.

. . .

•••

Table of Contents

◦ ◦ ◦

• • •

• • •

Prologue

My "Ten Legged Journey" began as a blog. When faced with grief and sorrow, a writer turns to what she knows best: words. Journaling my journey helped lighten the burden. I hope this book lightens the journey of those travelling down that same path now.

I called it "ten legged" because of the two four-legged Pomeranians making the journey with me—their four paws and my two feet (and our three hearts). As time passed, another four paws decided it was his time to join my journey. Since beginning this blog, four of my closest friends have departed for a place where disease and pain do not exist. It is only here on earth that our hearts feel the pain of loss once they depart.

This journal is not one of complete sorrow, for my days living with all of them could never be sorrowful. Each day, their faces brought joy to my heart. Each smiling face and day with them will be remembered in my heart always. It seems the bigger grief holes etched into my heart only allow more space for furry beings to come inside and stay forever.

Beginning Steps

Today is the winter solstice, the shortest day of the year. And today will be the last day of a lengthy but too short life for one of my own......a grumpy old man who inhabits the body of my Pomeranian, Tad.

If you read my books, you know Tad. Rescued three years ago, at about the age of fourteen, Tad has seen horrors few endure on his earthly journey. Now, he prepares for a journey to join his brother, Ozzy. My little Thoreau will find Walden Pond tomorrow, with the help of a caring veterinarian and his mom at his side.

It has been a rough week, a week of tears. Bobby, my other eight-year-old Pomeranian, was diagnosed with lymphoma.

So, as most writers do when life becomes dark and hugs and conversation do not soothe, I reach for the pen or computer and write. I write to let the emotions I keep *penned up* inside flow and journey to the eyes and minds and hearts of readers—to the eyes and minds and hearts of those who might also walk this journey. All of us with pets will face our turn.

Tad has a neurological disease. When eating stopped and quality of life was nil, the vet said it would be time. That time has come. I have tried…..homemade feasts, fast food temptations, treats…..none has been taken. Life has become sleep, and that is all.

Tomorrow, the sleeper will awaken to a new journey…..like the journey he took three years ago to a different world. A world unlike the hoarder's home he knew, the sickness from which he almost perished, the fleas that infested each inch of his tiny body. Tomorrow, Walden Pond awaits…..his brother Ozzy waits.

I took one last photo today...he sleeps. We tried carpets, fleece pads, and dog beds, but Tad would have no part of any of them. I guess if you live fourteen years of your life on the metal rungs of a cage, a wooden floor by a space heater is paradise.

Bobby is doing well; my heart hopes his journey will be delayed. After all, it's Christmas and flights are backed up…..too many going home. I pray Bobby is not one of them, not for a while. He is on chemo; the vet said we had no choice. Without intervention, the disease would claim him in days, not months.

So, this blog will journey a quest—a quest to find the best life for my tiny boy, a boy who still waits each morning for a bite of toast. (Now his plate is sprinkled with turmeric to boost his fight, blueberries to strengthen his cells.) A journey to make others on the same path feel less alone, less overwhelmed. I hope it is a place for those to write comments and share experiences and know that eyes, hearts, and minds will be grateful.

Yes, on this shortest day of the year, a ten legged journey begins.....of a writer and two little Poms, each paw and foot walking into a new beginning. Please share this journey with friends who might be grateful, too.

(That's Bobby and me......I own a historic farmhouse in Gettysburg. We are waging a war on lymphoma....I knew there would be a use for that cannon one day...... :-))

Bobby and me at our Gettysburg farmhouse.

My Grumpy Old Man Takes His Final Journey Home to Walden Paradise

December 22, 2014

My Rainbow Bridge spans Walden Pond. Today, the pond has one more resident—my little Thoreau (Tad).

Tad passed peacefully. The euthanasia process is a two-step injection. First, a sedative is given. Tad stopped breathing after the sedative.

If you read my books on animals and spirituality, you will know the meaning of the phrase *one for one.* I grew up believing that the Universe can sometimes take one......*to save one.* I write of some stories in my books. I can only say that I have experienced this in my own life, and was raised as a young girl to acknowledge this as truth.

Today, I thank a grumpy old man who thought no one would ever bring him home and love him. We loved him for three years and three months. He thanked me today......perhaps leaving to *buy some time* for a very sick younger brother.

The Universe has many mysteries. Faith and belief in things not easily explained can comfort in the darkest of days.

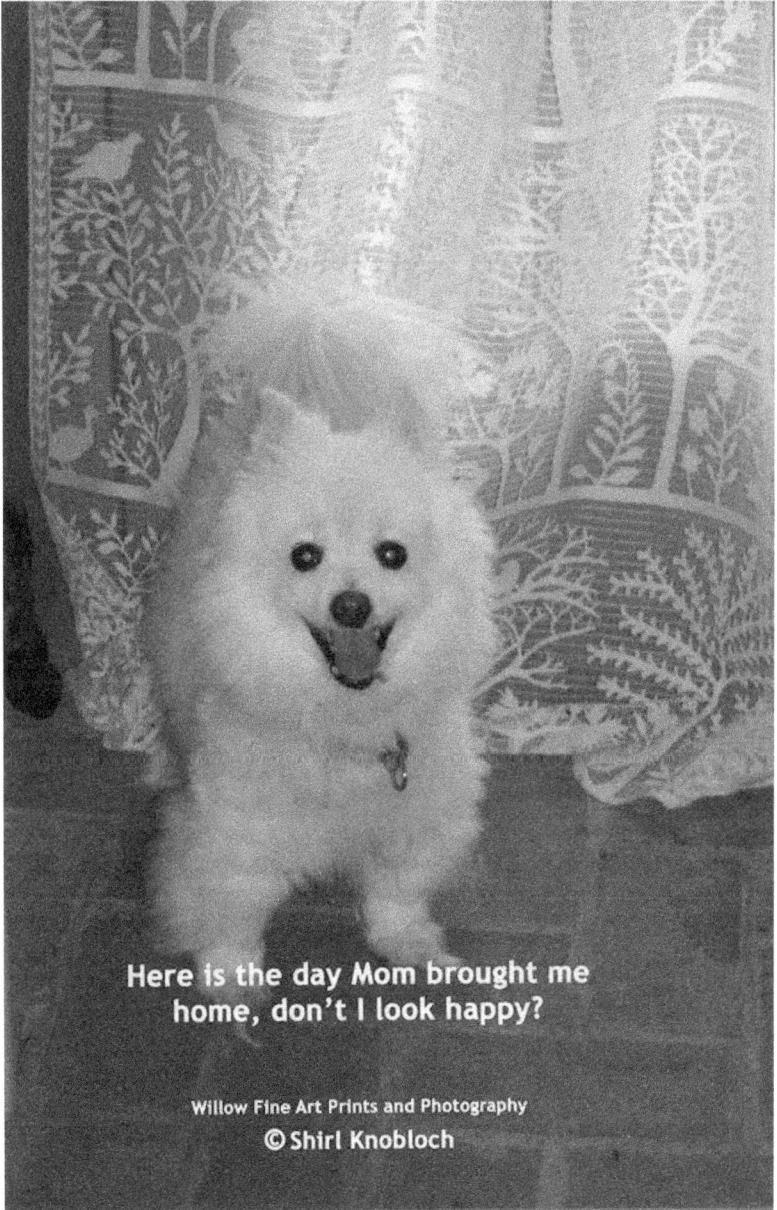

Here is the day Mom brought me
home, don't I look happy?

Willow Fine Art Prints and Photography
© Shirl Knobloch

Coping with Pet Loss and Grief

December 23, 2014

Perhaps the Rainbow Bridge is strung with lights, each one twinkling when a new soul reaches its path.

I think of all the twinkling moments this year......a lot of friends lost pets. Whether they crossed in April or December, it makes no difference......a year without a little one to tear at paper and ribbons and jump at the tree makes for a lonelier *first Christmas* for all who have given their hearts to an animal.

Losing a pet is the hardest of grief—second only to losing an immediate family member. Even the passing of grown siblings, seen a few times a year, talked to on the phone each month, does not stab at the heart like the empty chair or the empty food bowl waiting to be filled in the empty spaces of a pet owner's home. By no means does this diminish human loss; it only reveals the grief realized when *daily interaction of a loving pet* is absent. Some will argue over this.

There are two types of pet owners: those who leave a chain out in the yard to fasten to their *pet's* neck (and I use the word pet loosely here) and those who keep a running tab at the pet store, whose floors are strewn with toys, whose Halloween photos show embarrassed faces wearing witch hats...

I work with animals and owners immersed in grief. It is the pet talked to every day, the one who greets at the door, the one who shares a tasty tidbit at each meal......it is that pet who is dearly missed. We talk to family, co-workers, and friends each day, but we share our secrets with pets. We cry in front of them, curse the world in front of them, act like *fools* in front of them, talking baby talk and twirling them in our dancing arms.

Yes, it is our pets who stab our hearts with Cupid's arrow of love......and finally Hell's arrow of grief.

Waging a War

December 24, 2014

I looked down at my fingers in the supermarket parking lot the other day. In the afternoon sun, I had a panic moment—three fingers on my left hand were yellow.

Yellow!!! I hadn't been painting (I do work as an artist).

Did I touch something in the store???

There they were, a bright canary yellow…….

Then, it dawned on me…….I have been sprinkling turmeric on Bobby's food.   Turmeric is supposed to be a powerful antioxidant to help him fight the lymphoma. Turmeric is very *colorful*; along with my fingers, my kitchen counter has also taken on a golden hue where I have sprinkled it. I also give Bobby blueberries. There is a slight mustache (like the *Got Milk?* one) on the fur around his mouth……only it is blue. The dried blueberries seem to be very potent in the color department. I shared some and developed quite a blue-tinged tongue myself. Even my teeth seemed "bluer." Bobby has only a few teeth, so he doesn't have to worry……his tongue did make him look like a toy chow though. (Chows have those distinctive blue tongues.)

I don't care what color of the rainbow Bobby and I display—as long as it keeps that Rainbow of the Bridge far away in the distance.

Hoping our Christmas is merry, bright, and *not so white*....... *:-)*

Blessings and Merry Christmas Everyone!

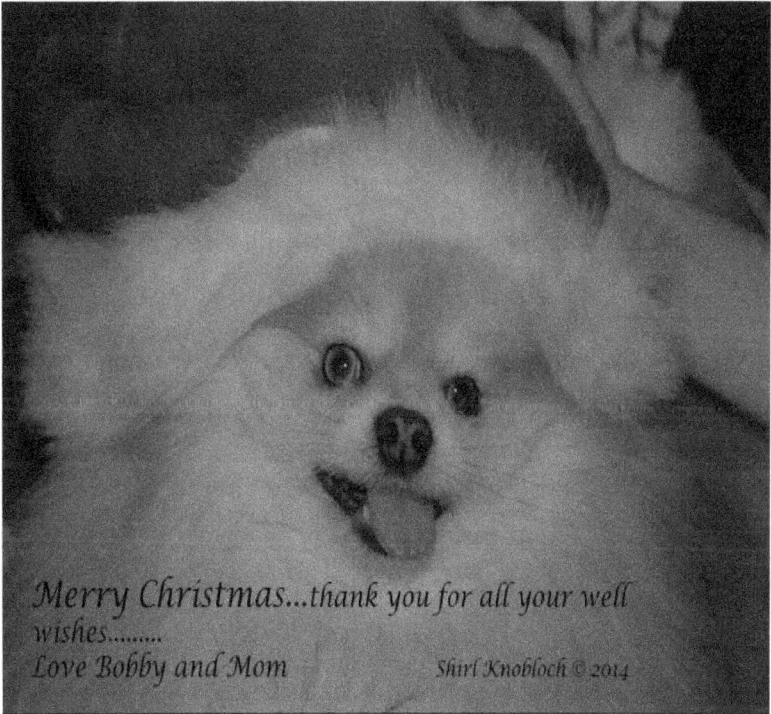

Merry Christmas...thank you for all your well wishes.........
Love Bobby and Mom   Shirl Knobloch © 2014

Messages from a Furry Angel

The day after Tad crossed, things started happening. Normal things for me; weird stuff for many. Light bulbs started popping......we went through almost the entire first floor by Tuesday evening.

Monday night, *the night he passed*, my husband woke up two times to the smell of my natural mosquito oil repellent. I reek of the stuff from May to September. Bug energy must vibrate at my advanced speed; they love me. One bite can swell up to the size of a jawbreaker in minutes. Was Tad telling my husband *I am here,* or was my grumpy old man complaining that he had to smell this stuff for so many months of his life? My husband said the first floor reeked as bad as I did on a summer day.

Then, on Christmas Eve, we woke up to *both* lights in our refrigerator out. We went to the basement—that refrigerator was off, too. One by one, half the house was in blackout. My husband put new bulbs in and tripped the circuit breaker. The lights blinked on and off in a second. Then, the dread set in......what electrician is coming out on Christmas Eve, and what is he charging to do so?

It wasn't the circuit breaker. Everything is fine……what happened? We don't know. Maybe some momentary lapse because of moisture in the wires; it had been raining all week. Maybe a mischievous little angel having some Christmas fun……

I like to think the latter. Tad was a night owl; he slept all day and roamed the floors all night. We would awaken to use the bathroom, and there he would be, wide awake, peering at us in the dark.

Electrical energy and water seem to visit me intensely during times of heightened spirit activity. I like to think he still is there, peering at us from a spirit plane darkened to many eyes……but brightening to many more as the veil between existences thins.

Another note: The morning we brought Tad to the vet, the plumber was there on an emergency visit—the vet's pipe had sprung a leak in his office. The Angels were waiting for Tad…

Bringing Aura Lea Home

December 7, 2014

We brought a baby Irish Wolfhound home. I say "baby" in the widest stretch of that word. She already is too heavy for me to carry around. So now, she joins a pack of brothers. The only girl—and yet I am sure the one who will "rule the roost."

Shirl Knobloch ©2014

Henpecked

December 26, 2014

Those of you who read my other blog on WordPress, *The Roses and Thorns of Life,* know Bailey. Bailey is the *bad seed,* the alien Pom whose mother ship dropped him off some years ago to make his way to me and cause havoc in my home.

Well, I think it is safe to say that Bailey has met *his match.* Aura Lea has taken a shine to this bad boy........as girls often do. She took her time choosing her amor. She tried to sleep on Casper, but he wasn't having any part of it. She tried to chew Bud's ears and legs......my Clara Barton boy just stood there and took it. Then, she chose Bailey, and the match was set.

She follows him around, her face right up his Pom behind......he doesn't catch a break. She howls wolfie growls at him, screaming in his ear to play. Sometimes, he does. Sometimes, he just can't take it anymore and let's out a *leave me alone* bark. Aura runs away dejected, nibbling on Bud's ear momentarily, then seeking out the apple of her eye once again.

She follows him around outside, which is not so good a thing. Bailey has bad habits......right now, he is tunneling a hole behind our shed. I think he needs a convict's spoon to aid his escape. Poor Bailey just can't get a moment's peace. Yes, Karma is a splendid thing.

Winter Ghosts

Another Christmas past......this one was a quieter one, more somber. It was the type of Christmas when one sits and welcomes the "Ghosts of Christmas Past"—the family members, the pets, the friends who were part of all December 25ths and now remain as ghosts.

Each Christmas brings more than gifts under the tree......it brings more ghosts, more visitors in the mind upon which to reflect. Each friend, each family member, each beloved pet with unique memories, not just from December, but from the summers and autumns and springs of years past.

Winter is a time to reflect, to face the ghosts that haunt our minds. The ghosts that we keep burrowed away in safe haven while the sun shines will now find a welcoming darkness to reappear.

We must fact those *winter ghosts*, the good and the bad, and realize that all have come to us as a *gift*—a gift of wisdom, happiness, sadness...a gift of life. For that is what life brings........until all our ghosts unite.

If You're Heading for the Concrete, You're Going to Hit It

December 28, 2014

Yesterday was a bad day that capped off a bad month. I should have listened to my own intuition; sometimes, I still don't. It *irks* me when clients don't listen to my guidance, then head toward that same concrete wall and ask for the same guidance again.

We took Aura Lea, my Wolfhound puppy, for a walk yesterday. We got to the foot of the driveway when a loud Harley came by and scared the wits out of her. I told my husband, *"I have this fear she is going to break free from her collar."*

We settled her down, then decided to get her big brother to join the walk and guide the way. We had a nice time at the park and were just learning to heel at the street toward home. I glanced down and saw the leash in my hand…….somehow, we still don't know how, the leash clasp came undone and she was standing there, seconds before she realized she was free. (It was an expensive new leash. We still don't know how or why it happened, but that leash will never be used again.)

I made a dive bomb toward her and grasped her, but I lost my balance.......I made a hard landing on the pavement, still holding on to her as best I could until my husband came.

I am petite; Aura Lea already is a handful for me. The Angels must have been there. They must have said, *This girl has had enough. One dog dying three days before Christmas, another home with lymphoma.* Luckily, I got up. I am swollen, black and blue and bruised in many places, but not broken. I won't be running any marathons soon, or walking to the park for that matter, but it could have been worse. My hands could not break my fall as I held on to Aura Lea; I hit that concrete hard.

My husband let go of Aura Lea's brother in the process. He was casually crossing the busy street. In a half-shock daze, I saw him by himself across the street. The Angels were there, too. Had a car been coming, he would have been in real danger. *"I have to go get him,"* my husband said. So, I lay bleeding on the concrete, holding on to a Wolfhound pup for dear life. One hopes someone will be there to catch them as they fall. I know I certainly have watched my children and grandchildren fall and could not get to them in time to stop the descent. I am glad some Angels were there for me.

• • •

To paraphrase the words of another famous intuitive by the name of Newton........*If you are heading toward the concrete, you are going to hit it.* If you are very lucky, some Angels will soften it for you. I suffered a broken nose and a blow to my ego. Both took some time to heal.

A New Year's Smile

January 1, 2015

I didn't watch the ball drop last night. Bobby and I sat on the couch watching the PBS Lincoln Center Tribute to Gershwin. For me, that beats Rockin' Eve any day. Besides, I already *was* the New Year's Ball; I just fell a little early.

I never understood why thousands stand outside for 12 hours in freezing temperatures to get an *up-front* glimpse at a piece of crystal dropping from a pole. I don't like crowds, and the thought of being kissed by a half-drunk stranger is about the last thing on my bucket list of the Universe. Waking up this morning to the news of a New Year's Eve stampede on the other side of the globe was even more unfathomable.

So instead, I sat next to a little Pom who might not see another Lincoln Center New Year's Eve again. I sang him Gershwin songs.......*Mornin' time an' evenin' time an' summer time an' winter time.......Bobby, I's your mommy now.......*

And then we went to sleep. Tad was in my dream. It wasn't a dream about him; he was just *there*, looking up at me, smiling. And that, my friends, was more celebratory than a 1,000 New Year's Eve kisses from those I do not and never will love......

Resolutions

I don't make resolutions......I think most fall by the wayside.

I think our thoughts each day solidify our resolutions.........that longing inside to become your purpose in life is our *constant* resolution that follows from youth into old age.

For me, it was to write. It was always there.

A wise person once wrote that passions are smoldering fires inside—if you don't release them into the Universe, their smoke will suffocate. My writing smoldered inside until other paths in life had been "adventured." I have walked a George Plimpton-type life, never finding my niche, never quite fitting in, until.......

Writing fits me in. Words carry my fire into the Universe and clear away the smolder.

So if you make one resolution this January, be it to "clear away your smolder"........

And I will make one other—to keep Bobby as healthy and happy as his little body and the Universe allows.

Each Morning Hello

Each morning, Bobby barks hello to me. What once was routine has become a joy and a sorrow for me.

I think of the morning when I will not hear his bark as he waits for breakfast. I try not to let the thoughts of future silence deaden the sound of a high-pitched greeting from my little boy today. When I lay down on the sofa and he climbs on top to snuggle, my mind tries to concentrate on the moment, but my heart brings a line of tears upon my face.

So, on this January 9th, I remind myself to give thanks for a little bark and tail wagging in the morning cold.........before the cold of sorrow will be a thousand times worse than any winter wind can summon to my heart. There will be time enough for tears. Each day of happy barks will be treasured.........

Give thanks for the routine things—the tail wags, the slobbery licks, the fur on your black dress pants, or the crumbs on your kitchen floor........for so much can change in the blink of an eye or the little bark of a tiny friend.

"Bobby"

Shirl Knobloch ©

Bobby Update

Bobby is doing okay. He has had some minor side effects from the chemo and his appetite is a little diminished, but all in all, he is putting up a fight.

I took this photograph a couple of days ago. In my kitchen hang the words from the title song of *Babe,* "Ordinary Miracles."

I am hoping for a *not so Ordinary Miracle.* Perhaps the little orb in the picture is Bobby's guardian Angel bringing him one.

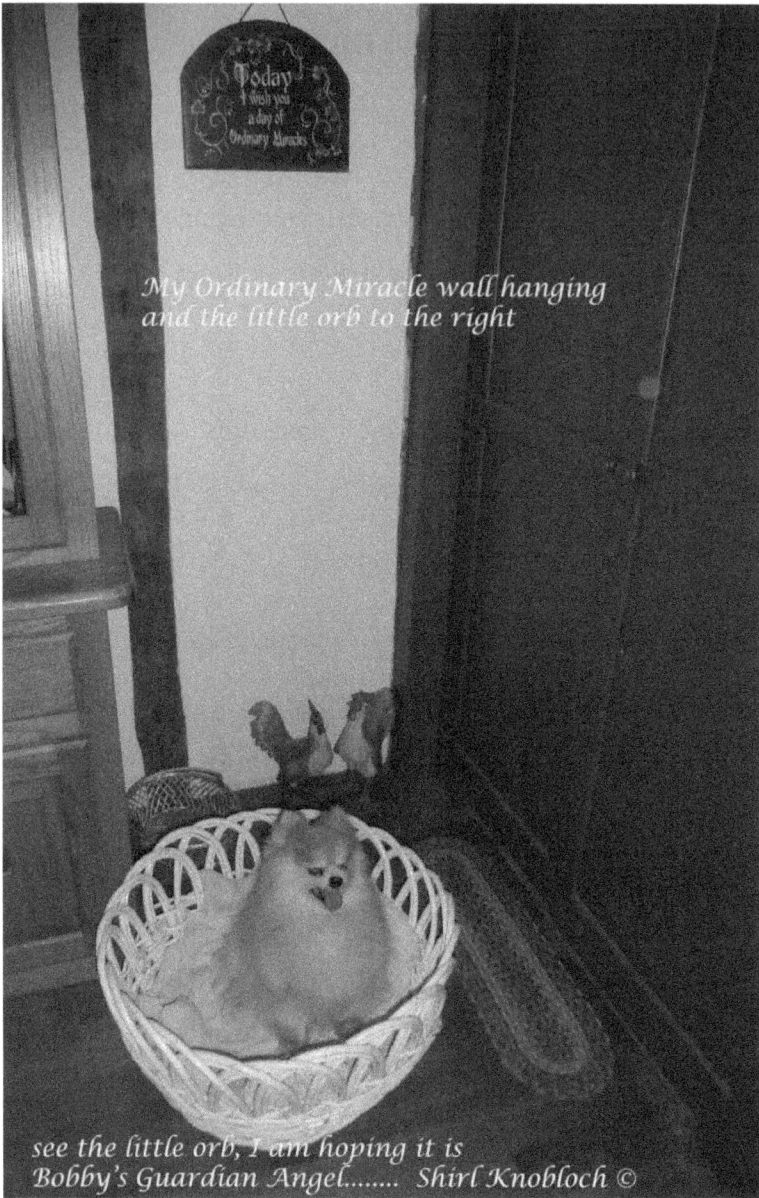

Today I wish you a day of Ordinary Miracles

My Ordinary Miracle wall hanging
and the little orb to the right

see the little orb, I am hoping it is
Bobby's Guardian Angel........ Shirl Knobloch ©

A Good Way to Die

A friend of a friend's tiny dog passed away last night. Tucked under the covers, she awoke to find him asleep...forever from this life.

Imagine her heart......but, if it be any comfort, can you not imagine a better way to cross, beside the body of a loved one, safe and snuggled warmly against the winter wind in your place of safety and rest?

Whether in bed or on the coldness of a veterinary table, losing them has no "good way"......there are *better ways*, better than being struck by a car, convulsing in pain, or starving in a back alley, but there are no *good ways*.

It seems too many friends have bid farewell in recent months......

There is no good way to bid farewell to a friend.........

In the Woods

February 4, 2015

Remission………it's a hopeful word. It means you're *out of the woods* for the moment. Chemo worked quickly for Bobby; he was out of the words right away.

But the vet warned against hopefulness……my heart began to imagine miracle cures and years of health ahead. But then, the dark forest loomed before us…………

Bobby is out of remission now. His tiny body must again fight against the deep and threatening *woods,* a denser woods that chemo will have trouble journeying through this time.

And my heart begins to imagine the worst………

Like a Wrecking Ball

A popular song keeps playing in my head. Having a Wolfhound puppy is like having a wrecking ball......

I don't think she has ever *walked* into the house, taken a *sip* of water, or grasped a piece of kibble daintily between her teeth. But despite it all, she is gentle. I can place my hands inside her mouth to claim the piece of stuffing she has chewed from her toy elephant. I can give her a tasty treat without her ever pouncing on my fingers, the way she pounces on her bowl.

And she has never ever hurt my little Bobby.........

She may be a wrecking ball, but she is a *gentle, giant, fur ball of puppy love................*

Now, the statues in my yard may beg to differ. There was a massacre out there last week. Two bunnies were decapitated, and an Angel was left with only one wing. Playtime with a wrecking ball can be hazardous.

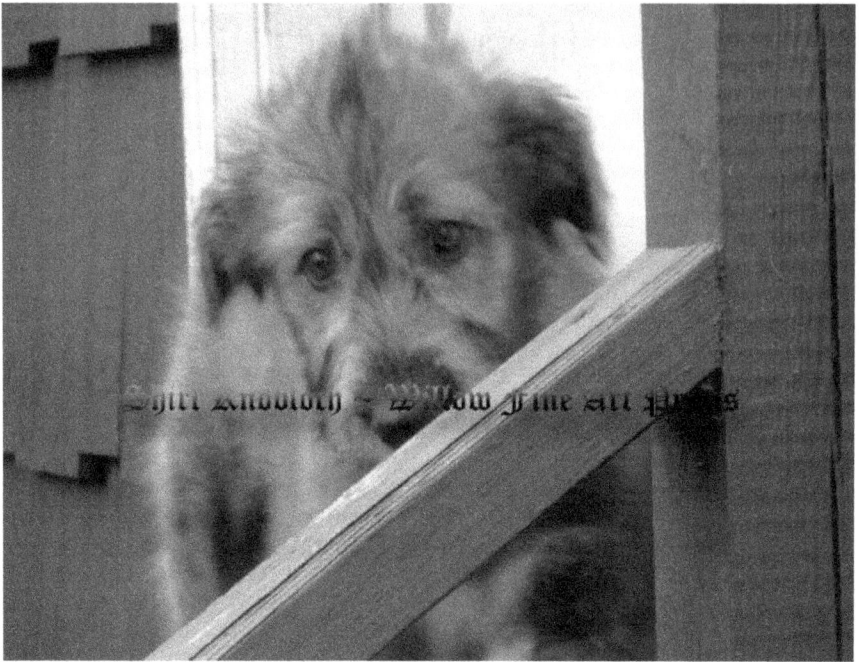

Shiri Zehbloth – Willow Fine Art Prints

Isn't It Ironic?

February 8, 2015

That song keeps playing in my head………

And that is what the vet said today………*It's ironic*………Bobby's lymph nodes are normal. His systemic lymphoma is in remission.

But……

Bobby has many growths on his neck and head.

Not lymph nodes. My boy has developed something so rare my vet has never seen it before. My boy has been attacked by a second lymphoma—lymphoma of the skin.

The bad news……skin lymphoma does not respond well to chemo. The good news……it is a slower demise….months.

More bad news……it is an ugly demise. Thankfully, the ugliness of cancer is most times hidden, shielded from our eyes. Not this one. As these growths progress, they will ulcerate. Bobby will lose fur. It will be ugly.

This is uncharted territory; we are trying medications and treatments, but there isn't a rulebook to follow for this one.

I ponder why, as the Universe always has a reason, though it is often shielded from our eyes. Maybe my boy's life and death will help teach how to heal other dogs and end the heartbreak for those who will one day hear the same words I heard in my vet's office this morning.

Isn't it ironic………….

As an added note………It did rain on my wedding day. In fact, a nor'easter blew in that day. If rain brings blessings, what does a nor'easter bring? It brings the gifts of so many furry companions to fill one's heart and home. Maybe that is how the phrase *raining cats and dogs* came to be.

We haven't given up. *Life has a funny way……….*

Bidding Farewell to Bobby

February 23, 2015

Bobby hasn't eaten since Saturday. I am trying......he is trying too.

But food, if taken at all, gets spit out of his mouth. Very rarely now does food even get *taken*; Bobby turns his head the other way.

If you follow this blog, you know he has been battling two separate types of lymphoma. We have combined conventional veterinary chemo with alternative supplements, but his tiny body has just been under overwhelming enemy attack.

Now, it looks like the battle is ending; he doesn't have the strength to get up anymore and walk around. A couple of days ago, I noticed his legs giving out from under his tiny body. Now, with no nourishment, his strength is weakening each hour.

I just walked into the living room and caught this moment. Perhaps it is the last time my little boy will look up at my camera lens. He was consoling Bud; this tiny boy with hardly any strength to move was consoling his brother and friend.

* * *

Bobby is dearly loved. He doesn't have a mean bone in his body. Losing him will be a dagger through my heart. Bud took my Apache Tears' death hard. She died from cancer two years ago this month. Now, he senses another friend will be leaving, and in one touching moment, I witnessed their farewells. Just look at these photos and tell me animals don't grieve......

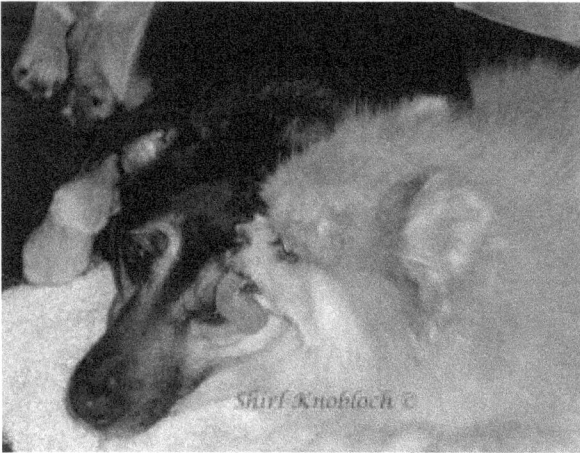

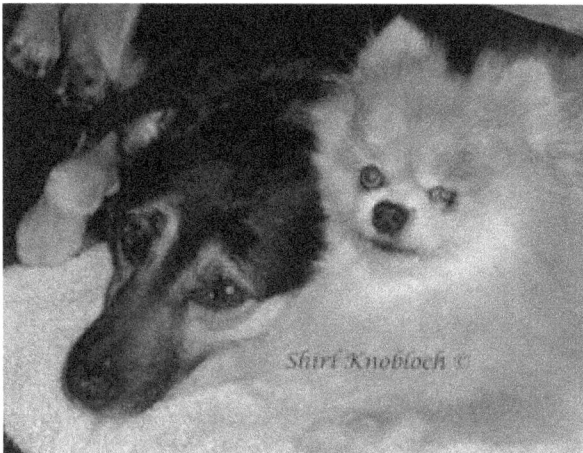

Henny Penny the Fart is Falling

February 24, 2015

Wolfhounds make their presence known in many ways......one of them, flatulence. A wolfie marks the air in a potent way. No one prepares you for this experience; I am sure all who own Wolfhounds will understand. I wish we could use that methane to fuel our home on these frigid nights...........

Which leads me to what happened the other evening. Aura Lea, my wolfie, was stretched out resting. Bailey, my Pom, had positioned himself in the hazardous proximity of her rear (actually, his head was inches away from her *bass......*)

Bailey is a drama queen. He can run for minutes through the house screaming if a twig gets caught in his fur. He is like one of those silent movie screen legends, the ones who take ten minutes to die, staggering and slumping over and milking their demise for more screen time.

I think you get the drift......or at least Bailey did of Aura's gas. He ran screaming through the house for a good ten minutes, literally gasping for air. Someone else would have panicked or called veterinary 911. Not us. We knew the drama queen would have to play this up to its full extreme. After nine minutes or so had elapsed, he was back sleeping in his treacherous position.

This morning, Bram and Bud were in the kitchen. Bram is a little Pom, my *Henny Penny.* Ever since he positioned himself at my feet while stocking the pantry and a deadly cereal box fell on him, Bram has been afraid of terrors from above. If I drop something in the kitchen, he *ducks and dashes.* You can drop a spoon and he panics.

This morning, in the kitchen, Bram and Bud came in to beg for some breakfast morsels. Bud let out a loud fart. Bram ducked and raced through the house. Bud had a guilty look on his face. I was in hysterics.

That is why I love them—in my house of misfits, amidst the heartbreaking sadness, there are always moments of laughter. My drama queen, my henny penny, and my wolfie air "freshener".........all helping ease the sadness of my heart.

Close Encounters of the Wolfie Kind

February 26, 2015

I have given up.........thrown in the towel.........

There was another casualty today, another harmless innocent massacred in the yard.

Beneath the snow, my garden now has more decapitations than the Tower of London. Statues that is.........from bunnies, to fairies to angels, they rest half buried in the snow, heads submerged, bare necks reaching toward the sun......

I guess that is just the way it is when you share your home with a goofy, clumsy, wolfie pup.

Come spring, there will be some gluing and cementing going on around here. Until then, the heads will rest, not on pikes around London Bridge, but in the snow of my pack's playground.

Bobby is still holding on, giving us more time to share with him before he chooses to find the true place where angels rest.

Don't worry, Bud and Aura Lea are just playing in the picture. Their encounters are more *bark* than *bite.*

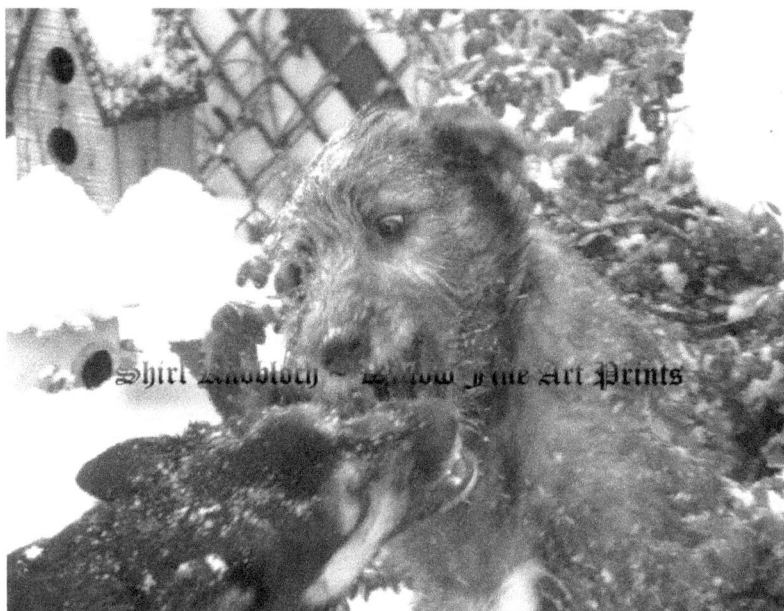

Shirl Knobloch ~ Window Pane Art Prints

We are physically helping Bobby to eat now. If he lingers until Monday, he will see our vet, and a decision will be made.........one of the hardest of my life.

Bobby's Vet Visit

March 3, 2015

As many of you know, we have been keeping Bobby going by feeding him with a syringe. With this help, his will to live has perked, and the vet and our family have decided to give him a little bit more time. He had another dose of chemotherapy today, and we are keeping him nourished until his desire for life and interaction with us deteriorates.

We thought the house would be a lot emptier tonight, but there is still one more bark, and we will take each night that destiny gives us. The vet said it could be soon, but soon can sometimes be longer than one expects..... <3

Keep sending prayers, Reiki, and strength. A few days ago, I would not have believed my boy would still be with us. I know all of your healing intentions really did make a difference for one little Pomeranian.

Good Bye

March 7, 2015

I have been lucky. I lost a toy poodle at the age of 12 to cancer, a sheltie at the age of 8, and now my little Bobby, who is nine. Other dogs of mine have been stricken, but in their senior years—a heart-breaking blow, but a softer and more *expected* one. Many of my friends have faced this heartache too often, too soon.

It seems to be happening so much now. So many of my friends' dogs are battling cancer now. My vet, during Bobby's last visit for chemotherapy, said cases come like ocean waves. This time happens to be bringing a lot to his office on the tide.

Why? Is it the food? I look around at the expensive "no grain" bags of dry food, the meats I buy and cook each week, the shelf of medicines on my kitchen counter, and the shelf of homemade turmeric paste in my refrigerator and shake my head. I shake my head at those pictures of grey, muzzled dogs, roaming the streets or tied to a chain, begging for crusts of bread. Why can some stay strong when others fall at tender ages, even though they are spoiled and nurtured with families they love?

Is it the vaccinations? Just that subject, both for humans and animals, can cause a head-shaking argument. Me, I go easy on vaccinations for my pets......I give what is needed in my opinion.

Is it toxins in our environment? My dogs don't go to dog parks; they walk on no pesticide-laden grass. Grass? That word doesn't apply to my back yard :-)

My point is, I don't know......no one knows this answer. But more of our pets are leaving us. They are leaving us too soon for an already too short life span.

And when you own a number of dogs, sooner or later the roulette wheel will land on this devastating slot......

It's still worth the gamble. It's worth every tear that will come after all the countless days of smiles.

My Little Dog, a Shadow at My Feet

March 10, 2015

"My little dog, a shadow at my feet." ~~~*Edith Wharton*

My ten legged journey is over. Now, eight legs walk in shadow at my feet.

First Tad, three days before Christmas. And today, my Bobby.

Deciding to end the suffering of a loved one is the hardest thing to do......for it is in ending theirs that ours begins.

It is we who are left behind and suffer, who feel the loss, the emptiness......the vacant spots where no shadow is cast.

Now, I feel like Peter Pan, and there is no fairy to sew my shadow back on.........

But my Bobby will suffer no more.

RIP My little dog, a constant shadow at my feet......2006- March 10, 2015.

Winged Angels (The Message of a Dream)

March 13, 2015

I have been deeply worried about Bobby since he passed. Bobby was truly my baby; he needed to be cared for differently than all my other dogs. He was too tiny to climb stairs, so we carried him. He would not go outside unless someone carried him down our ramp; then, he waited at the bottom until someone carried him back inside. He would have to be lifted onto our sofa; his little legs were too tiny to jump. And most nights, he would stare woefully at his food bowl until I hand fed each bite to him.

How would this tiny baby find his way alone to Rainbow Bridge?

I thought perhaps my Apache Tears or Tad or Little Guy would come for him. But last night, in a dream, I realized other angels did.

It was nighttime, pitch black. I was walking into my room and going to open the curtains to let the moonlight filter in. When I opened them, I gazed out into the full moon sky and saw countless beams of light moving toward me. At first, in the dream, I thought they were stars. Then, as they got closer, I saw them. Hundreds of white doves, flapping their wings, all coming closer and closer...more coming each minute. They all covered the night sky, like winged stars.

When I awoke, I realized the message in my dream.

I am a dove keeper. For many, many years, I have kept doves. This past year, several have passed in their natural cycle of life. I am left with only a few now. My house is much quieter now, with less dove coos and mournful calls and less barks to fill the emptiness.

Bobby knew the doves. He knew the morning calls, the sounds doves make as they open their tail feathers in mating dance to impress their partners.

Bobby would not be afraid of their calls; perhaps my doves would show him the path.

I now believe winged angels were waiting for my gentle, "furry" little dove......taking him home.

"Calling him home"

Shirl Knobloch ©

Finding the Right Vet

March 15, 2015

I have gone to the same veterinarian for over twenty years. He isn't just a vet anymore; he is a friend. He has watched my children grow into adults, with pets of their own in his care as well. He has seen so many of my animals come into my home and take their last breaths in his care.

Think about it. Who sees you at your heart's more raw moment, crying over the death of a loved one, besides family members, or perhaps a doctor or hospital staff member? Your vet. With whom do you place trust with one of your most cherished "possessions"? (And I use that term *loosely* since we do not own them; we only become their guardians for a while.)

How to find a good vet......

Word of mouth helps. Ask around. If you are new to the area, wander the pet store aisle and strike up conversations with people in there. They love their pets......

Look online for comments about a vet practice.

Finally, when you go in for your appointment, judge whether the vet is most interested in making money from your visit. Become knowledgeable about necessary vaccinations and tests. Pets are your children; just as you would not consider a procedure or test on your child without researching it first, do the same for the furry ones you love.

Is your veterinarian open to alternative and holistic ideas? Are they open to your disagreeing about a procedure or treatment, or do they make you feel as if your opinions aren't of value?

If your pet needs a specific surgery, look for certifications just as you would for a non-furry family member.

Notice if the vet "rushes" through your appointment. Does he/she take the time to answer your questions, or does he/she lead you and your pet back to the waiting room while you are still talking? You shouldn't feel as if you are *pestering* your vet during the office visit. You should feel comfortable asking him/her all the questions you need to.

These are all clues. We bare our hearts to our vets. We place those we love in their hands and care. Your veterinarian will become one of the most significant relationships in your life. My vet has shared some of the saddest moments of my life and the happiest. This has been a very sad few months for me; I had to help two of my best friends cross. Luckily, I had the help of a caring and trusted vet who went the extra miles to spend time with me through the hurt and tears.

Finally, if you have a good vet, don't take him/her for granted. I wrote a letter to my vet after Bobby died, thanking him for the way he took care of him. He cared for Bobby as he would have cared for his own pet, and I know he felt sorrow when there was no longer anything he could do but give him a peaceful death. And that is what my vet and I shared, Bobby's peaceful death......

Give Me Your Paw

March 18, 2015

Aura Lea has mastered the *"give me your paw"* command. Treats are a masterful incentive—so is cheese.

I just have to watch when she enthusiastically swipes that massive paw in my direction. She is almost as big as I am now, and stronger, which is a problem when she wants to snuggle in my lap.

Amusingly, when I am getting lunch or dinner ingredients ready on the counter, a big paw will suddenly plop down in very close proximity to the food. *"Well, you did teach me to give you my paw, didn't you?"* Large snout and wolfie eyes stare at the rewards waiting.

The other day, I was sitting at the computer when I felt a *lashing* to my back. It was Aura Lea's tail......

Expect to spend a good deal of time *soaked.* I call my Casper (a Collie) "Ladle Mouth" for the way his whole mouth sops up water, but Aura Lea is in a league of champions on this one. And what better way to top off that drink than to go directly to mom's lap and plop her wet mug in it?

No one could ever prepare you for life with a wolfie……no internet article, no breeder page, no wolfhound club or group.

Before they ever give you their paw, you have given them your heart………

A Peaceful Death

March 19, 2015

Frequent readers of my blogs know I am a dove keeper. I love these gentle beings......I have raised many types of birds over the years, but doves I find to be the most gentle, the most trusting of all. They trust me holding their babies and taking care of them when they are injured. They simply are the most beautiful of beings.

I have a pair of doves that I often write about. Their story is in my first book. I rescued them because they were tossed away. I later learned the reason why—each time they breed, the baby is either stillborn or born with a deformity in the legs and passes within a few months. Perhaps it is the result of a genetic problem or improper breeding, but they are a bonded couple for life, and to me, they are a treasure. What someone else thought a *zero money-making pair* is, to me, a priceless gift.

Today, they had two babies. One was weak and crossed soon after. The other is thriving but has the same leg deformity and will cross in a few months, too......

Today is Saint Joseph's Day. In the Catholic faith, Saint Joseph is the saint of *peaceful deaths*. *May these two babies each find a peaceful death.......one today, as I lay him in the ground, and one without too much suffering in his short time on earth.*

Musings on Grief

March 20, 2015

Grief is a fickle companion; he comes and goes. There are times you think you've gained composure and control, and then he steps right back in again to bring you to your knees. Waves of normalcy, then waves of grief to sweep you away with the tide.

It's a little over a week now since I lost my dog. My Bobby. Bobby was one of a kind; he had a lot of unique quirks about him. He liked to sit at my feet at night after dinner while I brushed my teeth. Tonight, an ordinary ritual turned into a wave of grief when I looked down and felt the emptiness beside me......

Everyone who has lost a pet or family member knows that emptiness. There are moments that bring the grief right back in your face, like a flash bulb bursting in front of your eyes.

Little moments. It's the little ones that get you, those ordinary routines that will never be the same again. Maybe it's taking a drive to bring your dad his dinner. Maybe it's wanting to share the latest episode of your favorite television show with a friend. Maybe it's wanting a little dog to sit at your feet while you brush your teeth.

Little moments......big emptiness......

Bobby's Phone Call

March 26, 2015

We were back at the vet yesterday. Bram, my other Pomeranian, had dental surgery a couple of weeks ago. Unfortunately, he developed a respiratory infection and is on antibiotics.

It was hard going back to the veterinarian so soon, just two weeks after Bobby's last visit. As we sat in the waiting room, I heard our vet on the phone with another pet owner. Hearing the conversation, I realized it was the other lymphoma patient's mom on the line. Her dog is being treated with the same medication used on Bobby. It was bittersweet; this dog was doing well—not in remission, but surviving. Good for his owner, but sad for us who lost our boy.

It was Bobby's lymphoma that precipitated the ordering of the medicine now being given to this other little dog. My Bobby was in total remission from the systemic lymphoma; the vet said he might have lived one more year for us. But the cutaneous lymphoma did him in. No treatment is successful when that rages angrily as it had in Bobby.

Bobby's pictures are hanging in the vet office. I wrote a letter telling the vet to let our boy help others going through this same sadness. Maybe that phone call, at just the moment when a broken-hearted mom was sitting in the waiting room, was a call from the Bridge...

Bram is doing much better today...and maybe I am too, after a *Rainbow Bridge hello* from my Bobby. My little shadow is still following at my feet; he was right beside me yesterday in that office.

"Bobby"

Playing Dead...Without the Bang

March 27, 2015

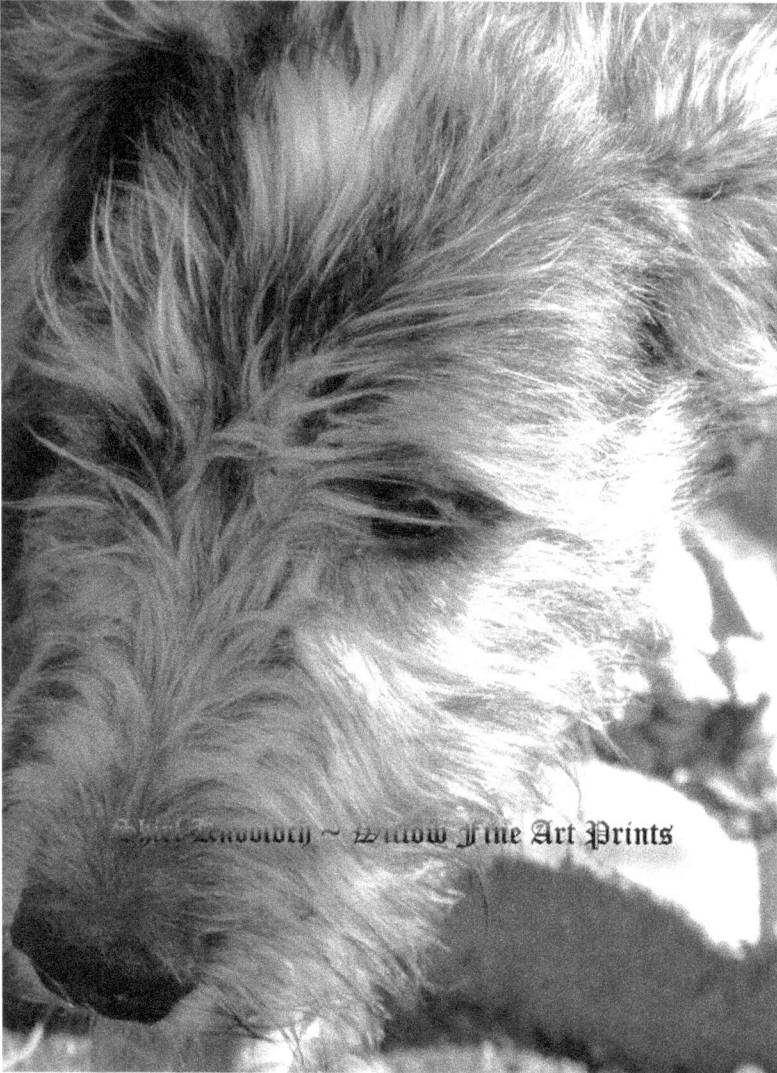

Photo Lenooiben ~ Willow Fine Art Prints

Aura Lea is almost six months old now......and growing each
day. I, on the other hand, hit the growth chart on the wall at

5'......and am now shrinking a little each year (sigh). As a result, training our wolfhound is high on our priority list. She is a good girl, thankfully—a little stubborn, but she sits, gives paw, waits if you tell her to......

But one trick we never taught comes naturally to her. When her massive puppy energy becomes overwhelming, it is time for puppy time out in her crate. When she was very small, she would walk right in, obediently. Now, at the very mention of the word crate, Aura Lea drops to the floor and *plays dead* in a heap. I cannot lift her, cannot drag her. The moment she realizes I have given up, she gets up and runs away.

Then, I say "crate" again, and you guessed it—a slumped heap of paws and fur, looking up at me as if to say, *"Just try and move me, Mom."*

As I have said before and will say again, thank God for cheese. I have the only dog that doesn't *play dead* for cheese but rather *springs back to life.............*

Wolfies, there really is no other dog quite like them.

Wolfies and Fruit

I just read an interesting post about wolfies and fruit. I haven't experimented much, but I know Aura Lea loves bananas.

Her taste is eclectic. Last evening, she was chewing on an arugula leaf that had dropped to the kitchen floor. She asks no questions, just opens her mouth and enjoys.

Anyway, the post I came across said wolfies like figs. Great, I planted a couple of baby fig trees last year. I am hoping they survived this tough winter.

Then, I read the next line.........*and fig leaves......*

Thoughts of chewed-off fig leaves and barren branches danced across my brain like sugar plums.

I can envision Aura Lea jumping up to my apple, pear, and peach trees to grasp some snack. My daughter has apple trees. Deer jump into the branches and knock the apples down, so I know this can (and most likely will) occur.

Well, better my trees than the fruit bowl on my kitchen counter. We are still learning *lady like etiquette* while dining. So far, she has been very good. She knows mom will eventually drop something, and she is right there with her mouth open.

Here's hoping mom gets at least one fig this summer..............

Bells of Remembrance

April 10, 2015

Yesterday marked the 150th anniversary of the Civil War's end. Bells were rung at participating churches at 3:15, ringing for four minutes, one minute for every year of the war.

I went back to the farmhouse yesterday. It has been a month since I went there. One month since Bobby left. I knew the trip back would not be easy. After a month, the pieces of his presence still linger at my NJ home; like the tide, they ebb and flow. Opening the door to my other home would send the tide raging in, and it did. Bobby's bed was there, his empty spot in the kitchen where I took his last picture at the farm......

One house of ghosts is enough; two houses are overwhelming.

We went into town to listen to the church bells. We parked at a space, and then at about 3:05, we moved on to another spot on Baltimore Street.

A woman came out of her house on Baltimore Street, walking a little Pom the same color as Bobby. He walked past the car, stopped at the tree, then walked on. From the back, he looked like my Bobby walking, and my tide of tears began.

So if you happened to be on Baltimore Street in Gettysburg yesterday and saw a woman crying in the car as the bells were ringing......

Well, grief is like the tide; it ebbs and flows with our remembrance......

Tick Days

May 2, 2015

Yesterday, we found our first tick of the season on Aura Lea. I hate those things. I wish I could start an opossum sanctuary at my farmhouse; opossums eat ticks.

Gettysburg has a lot of ticks. Not used to country living, ticks were a new and not so pleasant experience for me. I remember the first one on me. I was in my dining room at the farm and looked down to see this black thing crawling on my upper chest. Since then, I have had a couple of them on my pants legs. I usually avoid the tall grass like the plague during tick season.

My husband has been on several rounds of antibiotics.......

So, for other city folk who might be venturing into the country or the woods this spring and summer, I thought I might lend some advice.

First, if you can stay out of the tall grass, do so. If you cannot, then dress appropriately. Ladies, even if your figure is not *leggings friendly,* you can compensate with a longer tunic-style blouse. Tight fitting leggings make it hard for those pests to crawl up your legs. I go one step further. I wear boots. I don't care if it's 80 degrees outside, I wear boots.

White is my color of choice in summer. Don't wear black; you will never see a tick. Don't let people tell you it is only in the woods. I once had a tick climb onto my pants leg when I was walking on my gravel driveway.

Don't sit under trees. That rest in the shade might land you with a tick on your head. Yes, they do fall down from trees. My friends' heads have been visited while spending a moment under the shade of a welcoming tree on the battlefield.

I don't like pesticides, but I have to use them on my dogs. It is Just too hard to find every tick on a long-haired, dark furred dog, so the best attack is to kill the ones that find them. For me, I have tried all the natural oils......lemon, eucalyptus, tea tree, lavender, you name it. But if you don't wish to use the pesticides, the best thing is to dress smartly. Tuck your pants into socks, wear light colors, wear a hat, or maybe carry an opossum on your shoulder............ :-)

Me, I love the battlefield in the snow, and my boots still come in handy.

Knowledge is a Double Edged Sword

May 6, 2015

I read a lot.........always learning, seeking new information.

These recent months have led me to pages and pages of canine cancer information. Pages and pages of treatments, home remedies, herbs, spices, supplements......

I tried some with Bobby. I was waiting to pick up my grandson at school yesterday and heard a man touting the benefits of turmeric. Turmeric seems to be God's gift to the earth. I fed Bobby turmeric. I patted the paste on his tumors.   But sometimes, the anger of cancer is too much for even turmeric.

Too much reading can make your head spin. And it can make you remember all the little ones you lost before you knew as much. My Apache Tears was treated with thyroid issues for months before it became evident that it was truly cancer in her spine. A huge tumor grew on her leg, and she crossed within a couple of days.

If I had pushed the pages of knowledge just a little further, might I have saved her? One's mind filled with knowledge can be a constant ally or a constant foe. We cannot let our hearts feel our minds have *let us down*......man has written the old adage to justify this—"hindsight is 20/20." We always look upon the back roads of our life with *if I had only done this.* But, in reality, you can only do as much as you can during that particular part of your journey, and you have to place trust in those who possess more knowledge than you.

Ultimately, one must possess belief that *there is a time for everything, in every season.*

Flight to Heaven

May 9, 2015

The baby dove died today. Those of you who follow my writings know I raise doves. I have a rescued pair, thrown away because their babies are always born with the same deformity. This little one was born at the time of my Bobby's passing. He struggled to survive; it would be two months tomorrow for his short life.

He suffered. His parents tried until yesterday to feed him. He could not walk, could not perch to sleep beside them, and could not fly, though his wings would flap all night valiantly trying. He did not give up; he fought until the very end when he had no strength left to fight.

Today he soars. Today is the anniversary of my friend's passing......two years. I like to think she took his fragile body and led him to the sky.

A Spiderman Helmet

May 11, 2015

I went shopping with my grandson today for a bicycle helmet. We got a sharp looking Spiderman one......

Then, when I got home, I turned to my husband and said, "I think I need one. For in the house."

Last night, I was sitting on the sofa when Aura Lea climbed on next to me. Quietly watching TV, I was blindsided by a large head-butt to my own head, which is smaller than Aura Lea's.

I think I need my own Spiderman helmet.........

When you are tinier than your dog, you need a helmet, knee pads, and maybe a chainmail suit of armor......if not, expect to get a lot of black and blues, the price you pay for owning a 100 lb. plus dog that thinks she is a teacup poodle.

Sunbeams and Showers

July 16, 2015

For those who follow my blogs, you know I am an author and pack leader to a home of furry characters. Recent months have brought sorrow and goodbyes to two of them. Now, my Bram is very ill with heart disease. He is on several medications, but a genetic malformation of his trachea is posing a serious problem for his enlarged heart and making it difficult for him to breathe. On his bad days, it rains in my heart; on his good ones, a sunbeam breaks after the showers.

Through it all, he smiles every day and still makes me laugh. Add to the mix a goofy wolfhound, and it makes for some *America's Funniest Home Video* moments.

Aura Lea, my wolfhound, has grown so tall that I watched my Collie actually walk under her, between her legs, the other day. My Collie is a big boy; he tips the scales himself at slightly over 100 pounds. That should give you a picture of how tall Aura Lea's legs stand.

Bram, a Pomeranian, is so tiny that he gets into other problems around Aura Lea. He learned a hard lesson the other day—never stand next to the water bowl when your sister is drinking. I looked across the kitchen and saw a shower stream of water falling from Aura Lea's mouth onto Bram's head. Bram squinted his eyes and looked at me with confusion, his eyes asking, *"Is it raining today?"*

I wish I had a video......such moments are priceless, and soon, they will be even more priceless as Bram's journey to meet his brothers draws nearer each day.

Aura Lea usually has better "manners"; she uses my kitchen seat cushion to wipe her mouth. Sometimes, other *little beings* get in the way. One day, I watched her take a big drink, walk over to the cushion, and ponder for a few minutes what to do........as my three-year-old grandson was sitting on the kitchen chair at the time. Luckily, her brain calculated that wiping her mouth on my grandson would be the inappropriate thing to do, so she sulked away, her wet mouth dripping.

Living with this pack of comedians brightens the day, brightens the *shadowy* times of life. For now, Bram will make me laugh, his little head basking in the sunshine......or the showers of life. And so, too, my heart will bask..................

Shirl Knobloch ©

When Love Dies

August 2, 2015

My little pacific parrotlet girl died this morning. She was old; she lived a long life but lost her vitality due to old age.

She leaves behind a mate, bonded for almost two decades. It was so sad to see him nudging her each day, trying to make her walk and eat.......when all she wanted to do was sleep.

Birds bond very strongly and attack enemies just as passionately. Those who have read *Birdsong* know the story of my mated pair and the murderous end of one. But when one of the pair is sick and dying, the mated bird will spread its wings and envelope the other in a sorrowful embrace. They will sing and chirp for days afterward, calling to them.

I put the little girl in a box, showed it to him, and told her she had to leave.....so he would not look for her anymore.

Her head was bloodied—not due to attack, but by his endless pecking for her to *wake up*. Watching the mate left behind is one of the saddest things to see.......in any form of being.

He is too old to get a new mate. Frankly, I am too old too to commit to parrots that live for decades. He might bond again;

he might be rejected; he might attack a new girl. So, he will spend his remaining days alone with memories, much like the humans who love and lose and cage little birds.

Angered Grief

Most of you know I recently lost a pacific parrotlet, mated for almost two decades with another who is left behind now. Constant chattering has been replaced by serene silence. But the silence of grief is not serene.

My little girl would sleep in a fleece hammock, spending all her time in it as old age progressively took her strength. The male would not go in it, never would set foot inside. But he would perch on top and sit, like Lord of the Castle—or Fleece in this case.

Since she died, he has continued sitting on top......perhaps looking out for her to return. I showed him her still body and told him she could not stay, but aren't we all blinded by grief, hoping our loved ones will return?

I was away for the day yesterday. This morning, I found he had destroyed the blue fleece; he chewed it from its hooks and left it sadly dangling in the cage by one thread. Perhaps he now dangles on one foot, his other gone.......his chattering now silenced and shrouded in anger and grief.

Birds are extremely intelligent, and they display a range of emotions comparable to human companions. I have seen empathy, love, jealousy, rejection, fear, and now angered grief.

Hopefully, he will cope. He is too old for a new mate. Putting another mate in the cage would be iffy at best. He might hate her. Worse, he might like her and be rejected. I have seen that happen, and it is very heartbreaking to see unfold, as one dances and courts and tries to woo and one wants no part. Committing to another bird that lives for decades is something for the more young of years. He is in his winter......and I am not in my spring any longer as well.

Hopefully, he is working through all his stages of grief. A bird's heart is just as a human's, only tinier.

Halfway in the Light

August 12, 2015

There are times when the camera speaks to me, seems to look into my soul and capture my heart.

Today was one of them.

I went outside with Buddy and Bram, my little Pomeranian, to take some photos. Bram is leaving soon; he has a bad heart and fluid in his lungs.

Buddy lost *his best buddy* five months ago when Bobby, my other Pomeranian, died. Now, he will soon lose Bram.

He is here, but fading......entering the light......soon it will envelope him and take him on his journey.

Today, he is only halfway here...my happy boy, basking in the sun with his friend.

• • •

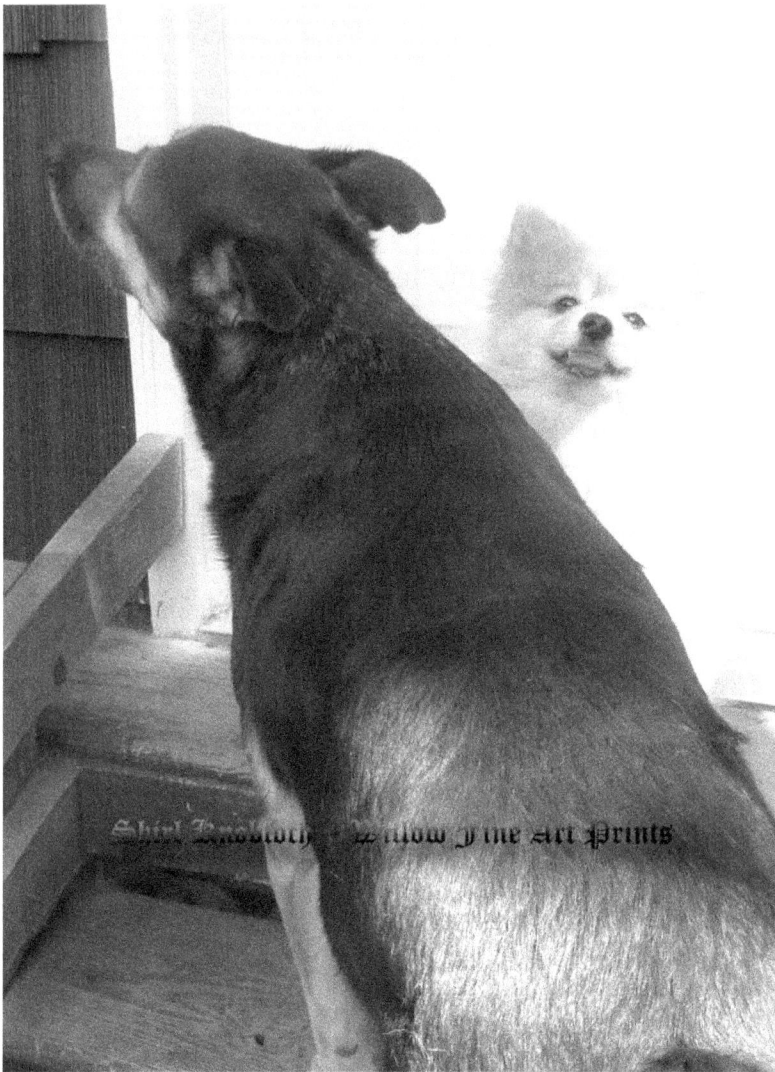

Shirl Knobloch ~ Willow Fine Art Prints

Just a Mutt

August 22, 2015

My Bud is a mutt—not a purebred anything, but a mixture of not quite sure what. We think doberman and shepherd. My vet thinks Australian shepherd. We have never done a DNA test. To us, Bud is pedigree, the pure of heart.

A kinder soul you could never meet in palaces or on the streets. In my first book, I introduced him as my Clara Barton. If someone in the house is hurt, you can rest assured that Bud's saliva will be all over them. If healing spit could cure, my Bobby's tumors would have disappeared.

Bud misses Bobby. He was Bud's best friend. They slept snuggled together on the couch each night. Bud feels it most when friends leave. When my Apache Tears crossed, he slept on her blanket the first few nights.

Bud is the one that gets taken advantage of because he lets it be. I have never heard a growl pass from his lips, even as cookies or food are being snatched by another.

The other evening, around eleven, my husband let Bud outside. When he opened the back door and called him to come in, Bud didn't stir. He was curled up in a ball at the base of our ramp. (We have a ramp for all the elderly or arthritic dogs we have rescued.)

My husband feared Bud was hurt. On closer inspection, he saw Bud cuddled next to a baby opossum. I am sure that opossum must have curled in a ball out of fear. I am also sure that the baby opossum went home to his mama with a lot of dog saliva covering his fur. My Bud doesn't have a mean bone in his body. Clara couldn't hurt anything……….anything except a pesky fly. (Bud has been known to catch those in his mouth. Hey, a guy's gotta have a special treat every once in a while!)

Buddy is my own gentle Shrek (as you can see from the picture). He had a hard beginning, being rescued just before his last hours were up at a kill shelter in Virginia. That car ride to NJ contained priceless cargo, the sweetest dog imaginable. When I read of all those who don't make it out, I know there are so many Buds who never got to share their saliva and love with anymore, and that makes me very, very sad……………

Giving Your Heart to an Irish Wolfhound

September 8, 2015

Aura Lea turns one next month. Sometimes, I think about that........one out of a possible eight or ten years at best. For so many wolfhounds, much shorter. I read posts from other owners who have lost their hounds at only three. That scares me.....one gone out of three.

When I first talked to my veterinarian about getting a wolfhound, he asked, "You do know their life span, don't you?" I did. I had been lucky with dogs that lived over ten years. But, as in all areas of life, luck shifts. This past year, I lost a beloved Pomeranian, Bobby, only halfway through his expected life span. I lost a sheltie at only eight from cancer, as well. My other Pomeranian, Bram, is terminally ill with advanced heart disease, and he is only middle aged. Life offers no promises, no guarantees that dogs supposed to live fifteen years will, or that dogs supposed to cross much sooner will.

Your heart breaks. Whether they live to be eight months or eight years.......or, if you are very lucky, a very white-faced old soul walks slowly beside you.

Each time I read of a friend's wolfhound passing, that same fear returns for a moment. All our lives are moments really in the Universe of time. We have to enjoy each one, each year.

Next month, Aura Lea will have two candles on her cake, one for her birthday and one for luck to grow on......to grow on as long as this Universe allows.

The Heart's Choice

October 5, 2015

Through the years, I have seen many friends cross. I have held many pets in my arms as they took their final breaths. Other times, I have awakened to a quiet, lifeless body, not a barking, wagging tail. Some have gone quickly and unexpectedly; others have endured pain and suffering.

My thoughts on death have changed with the years as well. My heart used to cling to each added day, every next morning, wanting as many as fate would allow. Thankfully, I didn't have to euthanize any of my pets until only a few years ago, when I had to make the decision to end my Little Guy's suffering. I had fed him with an eyedropper for eleven days after a stroke. His body lay there at the end of the dropper, but he wasn't there anymore. It took my heart eleven days to make the choice. The vet said he rarely saw others with the patience to do what I had done.

Now I realize it wasn't patience; it was my heart's selfishness to hold on......

Watching my father die with whatever dignity he could grasp only made me realize this more. Letting them go or helping them go is the greatest blessing of the heart one can give.

Now my Bram is crossing the threshold called "quality of life." He has begun to let go, and my heart will decide when and if I must help him do this. Watching him suffer for an extra morning or extra day is (something I have learned only through growing older) not *of the heart.*

There are those who end the life of a pet for *convenience.* That choice has nothing to do with the heart. But to end the suffering of one whose heart is bound to yours………that is the hardest and greatest gift a heart can give.

(A couple of weeks ago, Bram and I celebrated Halloween a bit early. Here is the sweetest little warlock my heart has ever seen. My heart hopes he remains with me until Halloween, but if he cannot and needs my help, my heart will give it……because that is what my heart can do as one last gesture of my love.)

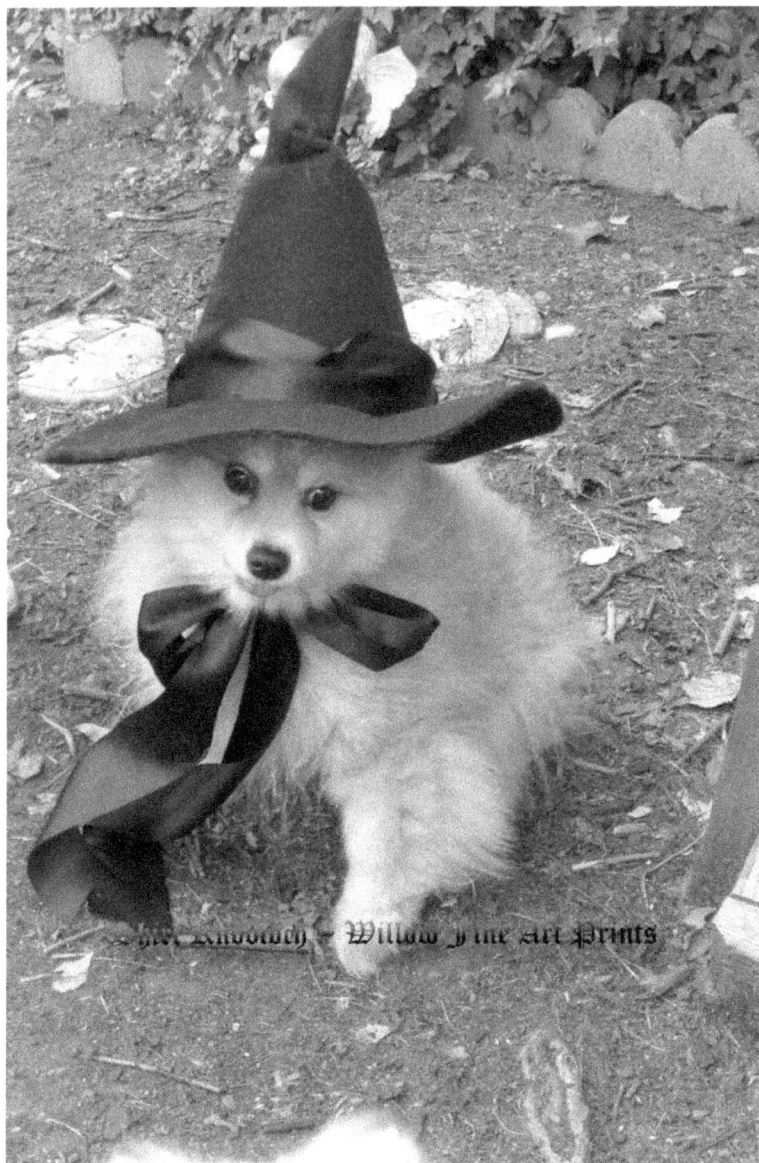

© Lee Knoernweh ~ Willow Fine Art Prints

Braveheart

October 17, 2015

My little dragon is fighting hard. Bram wasn't doing so well a week ago, but raising his medicine dosage has perked his dragon tail up a bit. I am grateful to be enjoying these Halloween season days with him.

Thank you all for sending my little boy extra "dragon strength."

,

Bittersweet October

This Halloween will be bittersweet. Last night, a very dear friend lost her dog to the same condition my Bram is battling. The vet gave Bram 3-6 months. Bram has just passed the 4th month. I look through veiled eyes, like we all do every day.

We look through veiled eyes for many different reasons. This time of year, we look at different Realms. We hope for the possibility of eternal life, we pray for souls who have crossed, and we search for messages and signs that life does continue. This Halloween, I look through veiled eyes of denial, knowing he is fading, but pushing that heartache further and further from my sight.

October lifts this veil. It opens the doorway, it lifts the heavy mist before our eyes. It joins those crossed and those still mortal by a bridge that opens and lets souls pass.

I keep looking at Bram with that heavy mist of denial, knowing he will be leaving, but still hoping that some miracle will give him years and years of time, for he is still a young dog.

Last night, Daisy, my friend's dog, lifted that mist a little earlier this Halloween. It gave me a clear view on time and months and journeys.

Bram will depart. I am grateful for each extra day, blessed for each extra month, but he will join Daisy and enter that doorway soon.

My friend Nancy's heart is broken. Her Halloween will not be the happy time of dressing dogs and taking pictures, for one will be absent.

My Halloween will be bittersweet, knowing my own Bram may soon be absent as well. Daisy now waits at the Bridge. May she have a blessed journey, but may she wait at that Bridge and help my Bram cross to his own family of dogs.

And may their reunion be the sweetest of all...........

Blessings to all this Hallowed of Seasons, especially to those whose October is bittersweet.

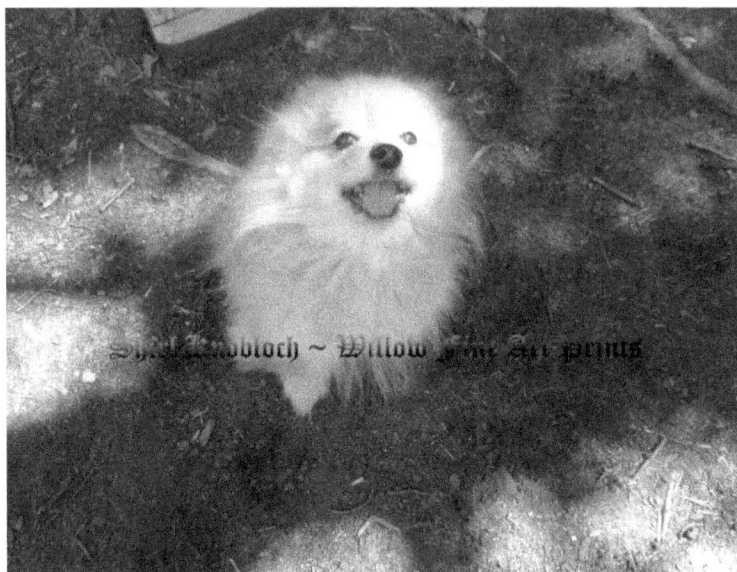

Shutterbloch ~ Willow Fine Art prints

Purging Grief

October 26, 2015

I threw up this morning. I should say vomited; it sounds better. But most say "I have to throw up" when that moment occurs.

I wasn't sick. I had my breakfast, got up from my chair, and threw up. I think it's been the horrors of this week. It seems so surreal to wake up and eat breakfast like a normal day after a friend of mine was murdered.

Her service was beautiful yesterday. I was afraid to go, afraid my energy would absorb too much darkness there. Autumn leaves fell; I collected some and have pressed them to keep.

I think my body was letting go, purging. I am a Reiki Master. When some study Reiki, they become ill with flu-like symptoms. They throw up. It is said it is like a detoxification of the darkness and blockage in one's energy, the body's way of clearing itself.

Maybe I didn't have enough darkness in me until this morning......

So many carry darkness. Sometimes, that anger and hurt festers and comes out in illness. Sometimes it comes out at the end of a machete, as what befell my friend.

I read a very well written article today. It said the worst thing you can say to someone is, "Some things are meant to happen." It further stated that some things just happen and they must be carried by those left behind.

A couple of years ago, I lost another dear friend to ALS. It wasn't meant to happen. Some things just happen and must be carried.

One may purge, but there are always traces left inside. One can only hold onto memories and laughter to keep those traces at bay, keep those traces pressed firmly (like my autumn leaves) within their soul.

The Battle Ends

February 6, 2016

Those who follow my posts or blogs know I said goodbye to my Bram two days ago. He wasn't showing the ugly devastation of the tumors on little Bobby's body, but his illness was just as grave, invading his sweet little heart and lungs.

It was perhaps the toughest goodbye of my life. I had two choices: I could choose to say goodbye while he still hid the gravity of his condition (one that would take him in a day or perhaps a week), or I could watch him perish in my arms from cardiac arrest or lung suffocation.

Other goodbyes have not been easier, for I loved them all. Perhaps they were just more *certain*. It is easier to be certain when the tumors on a dog have become black with dying tissue or when the body of a dog lies paralyzed after a stroke. When a dog lifts his head to look at you, that is the goodbye that takes your heart right along with his.

I chose to hold him as he peacefully joined his brother Bobby. The two of them took a big chunk of my heart along on their journey. I still cry now, wishing I had scooped him in my arms and whisked him out of the vet's office before the needle went in. But that would have been for my heart, not for his. And I would take the heart's blow to save his little heart from suffering because he loved me with all of his.

Mornings will be later now; he was my alarm clock. Those who read my first book know I called him "Paul Revere." He was a little ray of sunshine, his tail always wagging, his face always smiling. That is, until two days ago when he looked into my eyes with no sparkle left in his, only fear.

Today is a hard day for my heart. It is the third anniversary of another loved one's passing, Apache Tears. I watched her suffer; her death was sudden, unexpected, and horrible. The heart breaks no matter how they leave......they take a chunk of our heart with them every time.

"I Don't Cry in Public"

The day you left

I cried

Swollen eyes

Red nose

Heart cut open for strangers

Who listened

Heard the sobs

My public tears

My heart was screaming

NO

I changed my mind

Don't put the needle in

I'll scoop him in my arms

And take him home

He'll live

They waited

Those who didn't know me

Didn't know I don't cry

In public

They waited

To see the face

Leave the back door

Past the window

Of the waiting room

I pulled my hood up

Over my head

To hide my face

To hide the pain

To hide my tears

I don't cry in public

I cry alone

I tie up the skin

Around my heart

Like the strings

Of my hood

But my screams

Just as loud

Though no one listens

I don't cry in public

But I will cry for you

Forever.

Escape to Narnia, Curled Up Inside My Heart

February 11, 2016

I wish I could escape to Narnia for a while......have some Turkish Delight with the Snow Queen, communicate with Aslan...

Losing Bobby was hard, but I still had Bram to pick up and hold. Losing Bram has left my arms empty of tiny ones to hold. (Large dogs are loved in a different way. My heart misses the tiny ones. I love them all equally, but there is a difference in the love of a tiny dog who curls up inside your heart.)

It's been one week today since I said goodbye to Bram. I made my first trip back to the pet store two days ago. Seeing the special treats I bought especially for him (to coax him to take his medicines) was sad. Seeing the cute Easter bunny outfits was even sadder. Bram adorned numerous outfits and bore the humiliation and discomfort with a smile on his tiny face......all for me.

My heart sank as I realized I had no one small enough to dress anymore. Putting a size "small" Easter outfit on an Irish Wolfhound isn't possible, even in Narnia.

I went back to the pet store yesterday. I bought the tiny Easter bunny costume with the glittery sprinkles on it. Some would say, "Why?" My heart needed to bring it home, even though there is no one there to wear it. And maybe a little Pomeranian boy in spirit was watching with his tiny, smiling face, saying, "Mom, I wish I could still be your Easter bunny this spring"....................

Bram's Lullaby

A friend just called and made me remember something that might otherwise have slipped my mind. Last evening, I had just gotten into bed, trying to quiet my mind and not succeeding very well. I was thinking of my Bram, hoping he was all right and happy.

All of a sudden, a music box played. It was momentary, too quick to decipher a song, but unmistakably present in the room.

I instantly hoped my Bram was sending me a lullaby. I named him Bram, the same pronunciation as the composer, but for a distinct reason. When he was a baby, two little dark lines formed under his chin like fangs. When I saw them, Bram popped out of my mouth......for Bram Stoker, the writer of *Dracula*.

The bedroom was dark. I wondered what music box was the source of the melody playing on my dresser. (I have several music boxes, but they are across the room on a shelf, not on the side of the room where I heard the song.) Not wanting to get up, I thought about it for a while and eventually reasoned that it must have been coming from one of the boxes on the bureau. I hadn't moved them or played them for quite some time, so I knew that wasn't the reason for my evening song. I fell asleep, and though I resolved to investigate the source of the song the next morning, I had forgotten until my friend asked me if any *sign* had come.

When I got off the phone, I went into the bedroom, wanting to see what song had played. There was no music box on that bureau. I know the sound came from the bureau, not from the other side of my bedroom. Could it have been my Bram's lullaby? I like to think so.

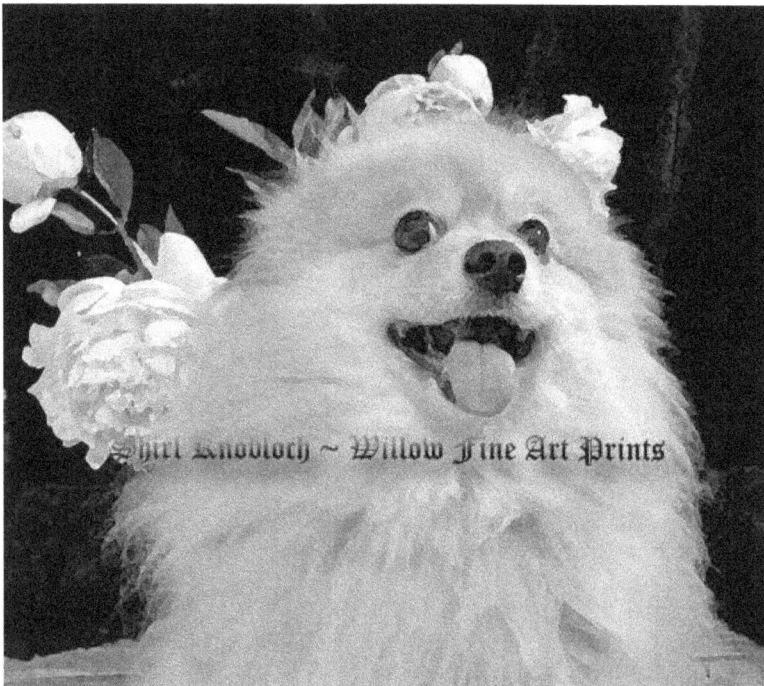

Spirit Knoblock ~ Willow Fine Art Prints

Epilogue

March 9, 2016

Tad has been gone a couple of years now. Bobby has been gone one year. Bram joined the two of them (and all the rest of his siblings) a month ago almost to the day.

Do I still cry? Yes. Grief is like the sea; it comes in waves. Sometimes, the tide is strong and washes the remains of memories right on the shore of your heart. Sometimes, the memories drift out on the horizon and bring some peace to the heart.

That is the price we pay for loving them. Each day, every one of my dogs writes a new chapter on my heart. That is one book I will never finish until we are all together again.

I wanted to end this journey with my favorite poem. Rudyard Kipling shares what all of us who have ever loved a dog feel inside our hearts.

"The Power of the Dog"—Rudyard Kipling

There is sorrow enough in the natural way
From men and women to fill our day;

But when we are certain of sorrow in store,
Why do we always arrange for more?
Brothers and sisters I bid you beware
Of giving your heart to a dog to tear.

Buy a pup and your money will buy
Love unflinching that cannot lie--
Perfect passion and worship fed
By a kick in the ribs or a pat on the head.
Nevertheless it is hardly fair
To risk your heart for a dog to tear.

When the fourteen years that nature permits
Are closing in asthma or tumors or fits
And the vet's unspoken prescription runs
To lethal chambers, or loaded guns.
Then you will find—it's your own affair
But--you've given your heart to a dog to tear.

When the body that lived at your single will
When the whimper of welcome is stilled (how still!)
When the spirit that answered your every mood
Is gone--wherever it goes--for good,
You still discover how much you care
And will give your heart to a dog to tear.

• • •

We've sorrow enough in the natural way

When it comes to burying Christian clay.

Our loves are not given, but only lent,

At compound interest of cent per cent.

Though it is not always the case, I believe,

That the longer we've kept 'em the more do we grieve;

For when debts are payable, right or wrong,

A short time loan is as bad as a long--

So why in Heaven (before we are there)

Should we give our hearts to a dog to tear?

Coda

I held my Collie's head in my hands as the vet enabled his struggling breaths to cease. I could never have imagined I would be here in this horrible moment again so soon after saying goodbye to Bram.

Casper was a very large Collie. He had just turned nine years of age. I knew his life span would be shorter than a Pomeranian's, but then again, my little Poms only lived to be middle aged. He was my beloved shadow, always at my side.

Mast cell cancer had spread into all segments of his lung tissue, slowly usurping all the space for oxygen. He was in pain, struggling to stand, and there was no hope of any treatment to make him better. The vet said he might exist two or three more days, in pain. Exist not as himself, but as a disease ridden shadow of himself, gasping for each breath until the final one took him.

I made the decision, the third one in such a short time. I still was grieving Bram. But this wasn't about me or my heart; it was about him and his pain. I held his head in my arms and told him how much I loved him. I told him to find me again one day. And then my heart disintegrated.

This time I couldn't bear to listen to the vet speech, *you did the right thing*, anymore. Hearing you did the right thing doesn't help a crumbling heart. I sat in the car by myself as my husband handled the paperwork and payment.

This happened so quickly. The cancer spread with a vengeance, taking another piece of my heart. Maybe it is a nightmare, caused by the grief of Bram and Bobby. Maybe I will wake.

The ride home is long, quiet. A large white cross is following us home in the sky for miles. Perhaps Casper has already gone to the sky.

April 20, 2016

The emptiness is overwhelming. When a little dog leaves, you can try to avoid the corners they favored, albeit without too much success. But when a large dog leaves, the emptiness envelops you. It follows you from room to room. I tried to sit in the yard, but that was worse. He always stayed at my side in the yard. Now there is just a void that cannot be filled. I am too old to fill up my house anymore. I am too old for a broken heart to heal. I will continue, but the house will remain emptier, less full of Pom accidents on the floor, but less full of their adorable little faces staring up at me. I can never replace the true friendship and loyalty of Casper. He was my boy from his first day at my side to his last breath in my arms.

I cannot escape the sorrow. I write. I clean out dusty old boxes of books. I find a tiny book about the loss of a pet that I had forgotten I had. It is years old and never opened. Enclosed in the back flap is a CD of songs about pet grief. I play the songs about dogs running at the Bridge and catching balls on the Moon. Someone else would think them stupid, but someone with a hole in her heart who lost her best friend yesterday finds comfort in the words. One of the songs says, *"I wait for a sign."* I wait for a sign. Perhaps this book and CD were Casper's sign to me.

April 21, 2016

It is impossible to understand *"the power of the dog"* until you have lived through the heartbreak from losing one. They have given my heart its moments of complete joy, and they have crumbled my heart into pieces upon their deaths.

To any who read these pages, I know words cannot heal a crumbling heart. Words cannot fill up the emptiness in one's quiet home. Words are easy to write, but hearts are slow to heal, and sometimes they never fully do. But hope must survive. Hope that they are waiting, someplace in another dimension, another realm or existence, to completely dissolve the one pain they inflicted on our hearts......their deaths. That pain will be dissolved with one lick, one extended paw, one tail wag, one bark...welcoming us home.

Casper was a white Collie, hence his name (for a childhood favorite ghost of mine). His spirit is welcome here. He can remain as my ghostly guardian until my days are finished and my journey to the sky commences. Or, he can travel ahead and wait with Bobby, Bram, and all his other siblings. When my last spark of life is extinguished, I long to see a sea of fur waiting for me in the light. Then, my heart will be healed.

Obsidian

There is only one crayon in my box today......

Deep, dark, obsidian black

Perhaps I shall draw a massive black mountain

A giant black bear scaling its heights......

Perhaps I shall draw a stark, black tree of winter...

A giant black raven winging from its branches......

Perhaps I shall draw a massive, black hole in the sky

That has swallowed my sun

And given birth to seventy-eight tiny stars......

Seventy-eight tiny outlines

Waiting to be filled

With white...

But not today.........

For there is only one crayon in my box.........

It is one week today since Casper left me. My heart aches for Buddy, my mixed breed shepherd. He was rescued from death row at the eleventh hour. Perhaps he has seen many deaths in his life and knows the emotions of fear and grief associated with it. He feels grief the hardest. My sensitive boy has lost four friends in so short a time. Buddy loved Bobby dearly, and he grew very close to Casper toward the end.

He seems to know when final days are imminent. During his last week, Casper took to sleeping in the kitchen. Buddy has slept in there since he left, which is very unusual for him. I like to believe he does not sleep alone and feels my boy beside him. Buddy never slept in the kitchen before, not in all the years he has lived here. In all the rooms of my home, the kitchen has always been the portal place, where spirit energy enters. Now, a Collie enters in the dark and lays beside my grieving boy.

Animals are so extraordinary; they see and know so much more than humans do. Grief envelops the hearts of humans and animals alike, and love heals both hearts as well. We don't walk alone on this journey. Furry paws stride aside ours before their final steps, and furry legs continue unseen to guide our path. If we believe, we can lean on them. We can make them our walking sticks, share the heavy burden upon their loving shoulders. Their purpose in life is to love us, and through my work as an animal communicator, I have come to understand their purpose in death is to see we are at peace.

Death is not the final destination; it is only a stop along the way. No Global Positioning Satellite system works with the precision of our heart. When our time comes, we will find them. They have been waiting for us. Sometimes, they even come for momentary visits, perhaps on a kitchen floor in the darkness.

Blessings,
Shirl

This is the last photograph I took of Casper...it looks like he is

already wearing his Angel wings.

He will always be my Angel dog.

www.ingramcontent.com/pod-product-compliance
Lightning Source LLC
Chambersburg PA
CBHW031340040426
42443CB00006B/409